EVANGELISM
Academy

TERRY ECKERSLEY

British Library Cataloguing in Publication Data

A catalogue record for this book is available from the British Library

ISBN: 978-1-910719-30-5

Published for Terry Eckersley by Verité CM Limited
Unit 2, Martlets Way, Goring Business Park,
Goring-by-Sea, West Sussex BN12 4HF
+44 (0) 1903 241975
email: enquiries@veritecm.com
Web: www.veritecm.com

CONTENTS

WELCOME TO THE TERRY ECKERSLEY
EVANGELISM ACADEMY!

How then shall they call on Him in whom they have not believed? And how shall they believe in Him of whom they have not heard? And how shall they hear without a preacher? And how shall they preach unless they are sent? As it is written: 'How beautiful are the feet of those who preach the gospel of peace, who bring glad tidings of good things!'

Romans 10:14–15

INTRODUCTION

Who we are

We are committed in our ministry to doing the work of the evangelist: bringing the gospel to the whole world. Our heart is to spread the Good News far and wide, and to equip and empower fellow Christians in their evangelical endeavours.

What we do

Working with churches, ministries and individuals in the UK and around the world, we train and equip – both spiritually and practically – in all areas of evangelism. We explore who we are in Christ, what we have in him, and how to share this incredible revelation with others through forums such as:

1. Training in evangelism (this course!)
2. Outreach meetings
3. Sunday meetings
4. Invitational meetings
5. Revival meetings/campaigns
6. Church ministries, prison ministries, outreaches, etc.
7. Resources, books, DVDs, CDs, online, TV

Who this course is for

EVERY believer is called to do the work of an evangelist. But how do we do this effectively? Whether your struggle is a matter of personal confidence in how to share the Good News with one other person, or whether you desire to reach out further to your community or across the globe, but lack the resources or know-how, we can help you!

This course can be booked by individuals or groups as a stand-alone event or as part of a wider event or conference you may be organising. Your life as an empowered evangelist starts here!

About Terry Eckersley

 One of the UK's most loved and popular evangelists, Terry has been described as a tonic: humorous, high energy, yet still vulnerable and relational. Using the strong gift of encouragement placed in him, Terry shares the full gospel message that has so radically changed him: a miraculous testimony of healing and total redemption from brokenness, severe drug addiction and crime.

This transformation has seen him become a graduate of and speaker at two Bible colleges, further rising to become a CEO within the Christian charity and media sector, influencing and helping thousands worldwide.

Terry is a creative communicator with an instant appeal that transcends all cultures, people groups and denominations. His much-appreciated art of motivational faith, coupled with deep insight, helps people to discover spiritual vitality. His manner is at once humorous, friendly and deeply impacting – and opens the door to life, salvation and healing, in a demonstration of the incredible power of the Spirit. To date, Terry has completed countless speaking, media, radio and TV engagements at churches, conferences, towns, cities and prisons, in many countries across four continents. He is also a published author and musician!

Jill is a worship leader, singer, songwriter and featured writer, and often travels with Terry, supporting him at engagements – together they make a great team!

Terry is also an Ambassador for Compassion UK www.compassionuk. org/TerryEckersley and Associate Evangelist with J.John and Philo Trust. www.terryeckersley.co.uk

Commendations

'Terry Eckersley is a remarkable man who has achieved an extraordinary amount. Yet as he admits, all that he has done is because of a God who, through his astonishing grace, rescued him from life's depths and changed him completely. The fact that God can transform a man like Terry today greatly encourages me in sharing the gospel. May Terry's story similarly inspire you!'

Revd Canon J.John, Philo Trust
www.canonjjohn.com

'Terry Eckersley is a gift to people who have faith and those far from it. Effervescent, engaging and never ceasing in seeking to be an encouragement, both as a public speaker and in the everyday conversations and contacts of life, Terry carries something that impacts and influences for good.'

Phil Pye, Arena Church – Ilkeston & Mansfield,
Member of National Leadership Team of AOG
www.arenachurch.co.uk

Meeting Terry Eckersley for the first time is a bit like opening a can of cola after it's been shaken up and down for a few minutes!

To say Terry can come across as a bubbling, effervescent extrovert would be about right, but there's more to him than meets the eye. He's a deep-thinking and thoughtful man who knows his God, knows God loves people, and knows his calling is to reach them on God's behalf.

I read and enjoyed Terry's writing on evangelism whilst on a plane journey – listening to my wife witnessing to the woman on the seat next to her. It was a practical demonstration of what Terry was explaining in writing.

This book details the calling and practicalities of doing the work of an evangelist – which you'll find informative and beneficial. It's good to be coached by people who are further along the road than you on these things – so read it with an open mind and heart – and then get out there and put it into practice!

Bill Partington
Head of Affiliate Development
UCB Global Missions

CHAPTER ONE

WHAT IS AN EVANGELIST?

Oxford Dictionary

1. A person who *seeks* to *convert others* to the Christian *faith*, especially by public *preaching*
2. A *layperson* engaged in Christian *missionary* work
3. A *zealous* advocate of a *particular cause*
4. The *writer* of one of the four *Gospels* (Matthew, Mark, Luke or John)

Do you fall into any of these categories? (Obviously not number 4!)

The term 'evangelist' is mentioned three times in the New Testament.

> *Leaving the next day, we reached Caesarea and stayed at the house of Philip the evangelist, one of the Seven.* (Acts 21:8)

This was Philip who proclaimed the gospel in Samaria and who also proclaimed the gospel to the Ethiopian eunuch in Acts 8.

> *So Christ himself gave the apostles, the prophets, the evangelists, the pastors and teachers, to equip his people for works of service, so that the body of Christ may be built up until we all reach unity in the faith and in the knowledge of the Son of God and become mature, attaining to the whole measure of the fullness of Christ.* (Ephesians 4:11–13)

Here the evangelist is presented as an office within the church. Interestingly, in terms of hierarchy the evangelist sits above pastors and teachers. The apostle plants the church, the prophet directs the church, the evangelist gathers the people, the pastor cares for the people and the teacher teaches the people.

> *But you, keep your head in all situations, endure hardship, do the work of an evangelist, discharge all the duties of your ministry.* (2 Timothy 4:5)

This was St Paul's charge to Timothy, to do evangelistic work. So we can see here that although someone may not have the office of the evangelist, they do still produce evangelistic activity. There are others in the New Testament who did the work of an evangelist – the most famous being St Peter and St Paul – but they were not described as evangelists; in fact they were apostles.

CHAPTER TWO

SPIRITUAL GIFTS

Is evangelism a spiritual gift? Can someone have the gift of evangelism?

*We have different gifts, according to the grace given to each of us. If your gift is **prophesying**, then prophesy in accordance with your faith; if it is **serving**, then serve; if it is **teaching**, then teach; if it is **to encourage**, then give encouragement; if it is **giving**, then give generously; if it is to **lead**, do it diligently; if it is to **show mercy**, do it cheerfully.* (Romans 12:6–8)

*Now to each one the manifestation of the Spirit is given for the common good. To one there is given through the Spirit a **message of wisdom**, to another a **message of knowledge** by means of the same Spirit, to another **faith** by the same Spirit, to another gifts of **healing** by that one Spirit, to another **miraculous powers**, to another **prophecy,** to another **distinguishing between spirits**, to another **speaking in different kinds of tongues**, and to still another the **interpretation of tongues**. All these are the work of one and the same Spirit, and he distributes them to each one, just as he determines.* (1 Corinthians 12:7–11)

*Now you are the body of Christ, and each one of you is a part of it. And God has placed in the church first of all apostles, second prophets, third teachers, then **miracles**, then gifts of **healing**, of **helping**, of **guidance**, and of different kinds of **tongues**.*
(1 Corinthians 12:27–28)

As you can see, evangelism is not a spiritual gift. It is an outworking of one or more of the spiritual gifts stated above. We all should be able to present the gospel (evangelistic work) to one degree or another. The evangelist, however, is someone who *consistently* carries out this activity with positive results.

CHAPTER THREE

BIBLICAL EVANGELISTS

PHILIP

- scriptural knowledge
- authority through signs and wonders (anointing)
- baptism
- receiving the Holy Spirit
- personhood (married, Christian daughters)
- under the direction of the Spirit
- meeting a seeker where they are at

Those who had been scattered preached the word wherever they went. Philip went down to a city in Samaria and proclaimed the Messiah there. **When the crowds heard Philip and saw the signs he performed, they all paid close attention to what he said. For with shrieks, impure spirits came out of many, and many who were paralysed or lame were healed. So there was great joy in that city.**

Now for some time a man named Simon had practised sorcery in the city and amazed all the people of Samaria. He boasted that he was someone great, and all the people, both high and low, gave him their attention and exclaimed, 'This man is rightly called the Great Power of God.' They followed him because he had amazed them for a long time with his sorcery. **But when they believed Philip as he proclaimed the good news of the kingdom of God and the name of Jesus Christ, they were baptised, both men and women. Simon himself believed and was baptised. And he followed Philip everywhere, astonished by the great signs and miracles he saw.**

When the apostles in Jerusalem heard that Samaria had accepted the word of God, they sent Peter and John to Samaria. **When they arrived, they prayed for the new believers there that they might receive the Holy Spirit, because the Holy Spirit had not yet come on any of them; they had simply been baptised in the name of the Lord Jesus. Then Peter and John placed their hands on them, and they received the Holy Spirit.** *(Acts 8:4–17; 26–40)*

Now an angel of the Lord said to Philip, 'Go south to the road – the desert road – that goes down from Jerusalem to Gaza.' So he started out, *and on his way he met an Ethiopian eunuch, an important official in charge of all the treasury of the Kandake (which means 'queen of the Ethiopians'). This man had gone to Jerusalem to worship, and on his way home was sitting in his chariot reading the Book of Isaiah the prophet. The Spirit told Philip, 'Go to that chariot and stay near it.'*

Then Philip ran up to the chariot and heard the man reading Isaiah the prophet. **'Do you understand what you are reading?'** *Philip asked.*

'How can I,' he said, 'unless someone explains it to me?' So he invited Philip to come up and sit with him.

This is the passage of Scripture the eunuch was reading:

'He was led like a sheep to the slaughter, and as a lamb before its shearer is silent, so he did not open his mouth. In his humiliation he was deprived of justice. Who can speak of his descendants? For his life was taken from the earth.' The eunuch asked Philip, 'Tell me, please, who is the prophet talking about, himself or someone else?' **Then Philip began with that very passage of Scripture and told him the good news about Jesus.**

As they travelled along the road, they came to some water and the eunuch said, 'Look, here is water. What can stand in the way of my being baptised?' And he gave orders to stop the chariot. **Then both Philip and the eunuch went down into the water and Philip baptised him.** *When they came up out of the water, the Spirit of the Lord suddenly took Philip away, and the eunuch did not see him again, but went on his way rejoicing. Philip, however, appeared at Azotus and travelled about, preaching the gospel in all the towns until he reached Caesarea.*

We continued our voyage from Tyre and landed at Ptolemais, where we greeted the brothers and sisters and stayed with them for a day. Leaving the next day, we reached Caesarea and stayed at the house of **Philip the evangelist, one of the Seven.** *He had four unmarried daughters who prophesied.* (Acts 21:7–9)

While Philip is given the official title of 'the evangelist, one of the Seven', there are many other examples of people in the Bible still performing evangelical acts without being given a specific title.

PETER

- Explanation of signs and wonders
- Pentecost – Peter addressed what they were saying

'Therefore let all Israel be assured of this: God has made this Jesus, whom you crucified, both Lord and Messiah.' When the people heard this, they were cut to the heart and said to Peter and the other apostles, 'Brothers, what shall we do?'

Peter replied, **Repent and be baptised, every one of you, in the name of Jesus Christ for the forgiveness of your sins. And you will receive the gift of the Holy Spirit. The promise is for you and your children and for all who are far off – for all whom the Lord our God will call.'**

With many other words he warned them; and he pleaded with them, 'Save yourselves from this corrupt generation.' Those who accepted his message were baptised, and about three thousand were added to their number that day. (Acts 2:36–41)

Calling people to Christ through repentance is therefore the key message of the evangelist, followed by calling and mobilising others to do the same. Keeping this message central is essential.

- Healing and use of this sign/wonder to preach the gospel

    While the man held on to Peter and John, all the people were astonished and came running to them in the place called Solomon's Colonnade. When Peter saw this, he said to them: 'Fellow Israelites, why does this surprise you? Why do you stare at us as if by our own power or godliness we had made this man walk? The God of Abraham, Isaac and Jacob, the God of our fathers, has glorified his servant Jesus. You handed him over to be killed, and you disowned him before Pilate, though he had decided to let him go. You disowned the Holy and Righteous One and asked that a murderer be released to you. You killed the author of life, but God raised him from the dead. We are witnesses of this. By faith in the name of Jesus, this man whom you see and know was made strong. It is Jesus' name and the faith that comes through him that has completely healed him, as you can all see. (Acts 3:11–20)

    'Now, fellow Israelites, I know that you acted in ignorance, as did your leaders. But this is how God fulfilled what he had foretold through all the prophets, saying that his Messiah would suffer. **Repent, then, and turn to God, so that your sins may be wiped out, that times of refreshing may come from the Lord, and that he may send the Messiah, who has been appointed for you – even Jesus.**

Healing is part of the call of the ascension gift of evangelism; praying for the sick is a command. Apostolic power is evident in the evangelist and as we see here, the 'dinner bell' for the gospel.

- Salvation whilst Peter is preaching (anointing)

    'We are witnesses of everything he did in the country of the Jews and in Jerusalem. They killed him by hanging him on a cross,

but God raised him from the dead on the third day and caused him to be seen. He was not seen by all the people, but by witnesses whom God had already chosen – by us who ate and drank with him after he rose from the dead. He commanded us to preach to the people and to testify that he is the one whom God appointed as judge of the living and the dead. All the prophets testify about him that everyone who believes in him receives forgiveness of sins through his name.'

While Peter was still speaking these words, the Holy Spirit came on all who heard the message. The circumcised believers who had come with Peter were astonished that the gift of the Holy Spirit had been poured out even on Gentiles. For they heard them speaking in tongues and praising God. *Then Peter said, 'Surely no one can stand in the way of their being baptised with water. They have received the Holy Spirit just as we have.* (Acts 10:39–47)

PAUL

• The book of Acts tells of all of the preaching tours that Paul undertook. Here we will just look at what Paul said about his calling to preach the gospel.

I myself am convinced, my brothers and sisters, that you yourselves are full of goodness, filled with knowledge and competent to instruct one another. Yet I have written you quite boldly on some points to remind you of them again, because of the grace God gave me to be a minister of Christ Jesus to the Gentiles. **He gave me the priestly duty of proclaiming the gospel of God, so that the Gentiles** *might become an offering acceptable to God, sanctified by the Holy Spirit.*

Therefore I glory in Christ Jesus in my service to God. I will not venture to speak of anything except what Christ has accomplished through me in leading the Gentiles to obey God by what I have said and done – **by the power of signs and wonders, through the power of the Spirit of God.** *So from Jerusalem* *all the way around to Illyricum,* **I have fully proclaimed the gospel of Christ. It has always been my ambition to preach the gospel where Christ was not known,** *so that I would not be building on someone else's foundation. Rather, as it is written: 'Those who were not told about him will see, and those who have not heard will understand.'* (Romans 15:14–21)

Paul preached without pretence, without pride. He preached only the gospel, and was not focused on his own ability to deliver it. God uses us where, and as, we are. All wisdom comes not from us, but from God speaking through us, and the Holy Spirit translating the message into the hearts of those who have ears to hear. Our efforts – our words, our delivery – do not bring salvation: only the Living Word of God which speaks to hearts brings salvation.

> *For Christ did not send me to baptise, but to preach the gospel – not with wisdom and eloquence, lest the cross of Christ be emptied of its power.* (1 Corinthians 1:17)

> *Now when I went to Troas to preach the gospel of Christ and found that the Lord had opened a door for me.* (2 Corinthians 2:12)

BARNABAS

- graced for taking the gospel to the Gentiles
- laying on of hands
- led by the Holy Spirit
- authority to confirm and encourage the work others had been doing
- personhood

> *Now those who had been scattered by the persecution that broke out when Stephen was killed travelled as far as Phoenicia, Cyprus and Antioch, spreading the word only among Jews. Some of them, however, men from Cyprus and Cyrene, went to Antioch and began to speak to Greeks also, telling them the good news about the Lord Jesus. The Lord's hand was with them, and a great number of people believed and turned to the Lord. News of*

this reached the church in Jerusalem, and they sent Barnabas to Antioch. When he arrived and saw what the grace of God had done, he was glad and encouraged them all to remain true to the Lord with all their hearts. He was a good man, full of the Holy Spirit and faith, and a great number of people were brought to the Lord. (Acts 11:19–24)

While they were worshipping the Lord and fasting, the Holy Spirit said, 'Set apart for me Barnabas and Saul for the work to which I have called them.' So after they had fasted and prayed, they placed their hands on them and sent them off. The two of them, sent on their way by the Holy Spirit, went down to Seleucia and sailed from there to Cyprus. When they arrived at Salamis, they proclaimed the word of God in the Jewish synagogues. (Acts 13:2–5)

Then Paul and Barnabas answered them boldly: 'We had to speak the word of God to you first. Since you reject it and do not consider yourselves worthy of eternal life, we now turn to the Gentiles.' (Acts 13:46)

At Iconium Paul and Barnabas went as usual into the Jewish synagogue. There they spoke so effectively that a great number of Jews and Greeks believed. But the Jews who refused to believe stirred up the other Gentiles and poisoned their minds against the brothers. So Paul and Barnabas spent considerable time there, speaking boldly for the Lord, who confirmed the message of his grace by enabling them to perform signs and wonders. (Acts 14:1–3)

TIMOTHY

- encourager
- perseverance
- prepared for any type of reception of the word

We sent Timothy, who is our brother and co-worker in God's service in spreading the gospel of Christ, to strengthen and encourage you in your faith. (1 Thessalonians 3:2)

For the Son of God, Jesus Christ, who was preached among you by us – by me and Silas and Timothy – was not 'Yes' and 'No', but in him it has always been 'Yes'. (2 Corinthians 1:19)

But you, keep your head in all situations, endure hardship, do the work of an evangelist, discharge all the duties of your ministry. (2 Timothy 4:5)

ALL OTHER BELIEVERS

• unity in the Spirit – the Spirit responds to a group of united believers

• persecution often has a counter-effect: the word is spread further and to more people despite intense opposition

• boldness in bringing the message

On their release, Peter and John went back to their own people and reported all that the chief priests and the elders had said to them. When they heard this, they raised their voices together in prayer to God. 'Sovereign Lord,' they said, 'you made the heavens and the earth and the sea, and everything in them. You spoke by the Holy Spirit through the mouth of your servant, our father David: "Why do the nations rage and the peoples plot in vain? The kings of the earth rise up and the rulers band together against the Lord and against his anointed one." Indeed Herod and Pontius Pilate met together with the Gentiles and the people of Israel in this city to conspire against your holy servant Jesus, whom you anointed. They did what your power and will had decided beforehand should happen. Now, Lord, consider their threats and enable your servants to speak your word with great boldness. Stretch out your hand to heal and perform signs and wonders through the name of your holy servant Jesus.' (Acts 4:23–31)

After they prayed, the place where they were meeting was shaken. ***And they were all filled with the Holy Spirit and spoke the word of God boldly.***

Now those who had been scattered by the persecution that broke out when Stephen was killed travelled as far as Phoenicia, Cyprus and Antioch, spreading the word only among Jews. Some of them, however, men from Cyprus and Cyrene, went to Antioch and began to speak to Greeks also, telling them the good news about the Lord Jesus. The Lord's hand was with them, and a great number of people believed and turned to the Lord. (Acts 11:19–21)

CHAPTER FOUR

EVANGELISM IN THE 21st CENTURY

Platforms:

1. Media – TV, social media, websites, radio, magazines, books
   (e.g. God TV, Premier Radio, UCB, *Sorted* and *Liberti* magazines)
2. School ministries – holiday camps, visiting evangelists
   (e.g. Lindz West and 'Light')
3. Prison ministries – (e.g. Barry Woodward/Proclaim Trust,
   Prison Fellowship UK, Kairos Prison Ministry)
4. Events – music, drama, food, community, street evangelism,
   conferences (e.g. Soul Survivor, Spring Harvest, Hillsong Europe
   Conference)
5. Churches – really all churches preaching the gospel of Jesus Christ
   and encouraging congregants/members in the Great Commission!
6. Courses – (e.g. the Alpha Course)
7. Missions, ministries and charities – (e.g. Compassion, A21,
   All We Can, Salvation Army)

Models:

1. Church based – Ephesians 4 Model: Revive Church Hull,
   Generation Builders Ministries, Life Church Bradford, Hillsong,
   Soul Survivor, Jesus House, City Life Church International
2. Parachurch – Operation Mobilisation, YWAM, Scripture Union,
   The Navigators
3. Independent ministries – J.John and Philo Trust, Billy Graham
   Evangelistic Association UK

CHAPTER FIVE

EARNING A LIVING

Money, is it a dirty word?

> *Don't you know that those who serve in the temple get their food from the temple, and that those who serve at the altar share in what is offered on the altar? In the same way, the Lord has commanded that those who preach the gospel should receive their living from the gospel.* (1 Corinthians 9:13–14)

Paul here explicitly states that the Lord has commanded that those who preach the gospel should be remunerated.

As far as we can tell, however, Paul never exercised this right to remuneration from the people to whom he preached.

> *But I have not used any of these rights. And I am not writing this in the hope that you will do such things for me, for I would rather die than allow anyone to deprive me of this boast. For when I preach the gospel, I cannot boast, since I am compelled to preach. Woe to me if I do not preach the gospel! If I preach voluntarily, I have a reward; if not voluntarily, I am simply discharging the trust committed to me. **What then is my reward? Just this: that in preaching the gospel I may offer it free of charge, and so not make full use of my rights as a preacher of the gospel.*** (1 Corinthians 9:15–18)

This was obviously his choice. It seems Paul did not want to make money a stumbling block or a point of contention for his listeners. We can see other examples in the following passages.

> *But thanks be to God, who always leads us as captives in Christ's triumphal procession and uses us to spread the aroma of the*

knowledge of him everywhere. For we are to God the pleasing aroma of Christ among those who are being saved and those who are perishing. To the one we are an aroma that brings death; to the other, an aroma that brings life. And who is equal to such a task? ***Unlike so many, we do not peddle the word of God for profit.*** *On the contrary, in Christ we speak before God with sincerity, as those sent from God.* (2 Corinthians 2:14–17)

Just as a nursing mother cares for her children, so we cared for you. Because we loved you so much, we were delighted to share with you not only the gospel of God but our lives as well. ***Surely you remember, brothers and sisters, our toil and hardship; we worked night and day in order not to be a burden to anyone while we preached the gospel of God to you.*** (1 Thessalonians 2:7–9)

We do, however, see that Paul was supported by churches to preach to the unconverted.

I do not think I am in the least inferior to those 'super-apostles'. I may indeed be untrained as a speaker, but I do have knowledge. We have made this perfectly clear to you in every way. Was it a sin for me to lower myself in order to elevate you by preaching the gospel of God to you free of charge? ***I robbed other churches by receiving support from them so as to serve you.*** (2 Corinthians 11:5–8)

At first glance, Paul's comments may seem contradictory. In 1 Corinthians 9:15 he is saying that he has not availed himself of his rights to remuneration for preaching the gospel, but then in 2 Corinthians 11:8 he says that he has indeed taken money (willingly given). The key to the difference is the end of 2 Corinthians 11:8, 'so as to serve you'. The money that Paul did take was not payment for himself but offerings given for ministering to others. Throughout his epistles, however, Paul reiterates that it is completely acceptable and right for those dedicating their lives to sharing the gospel to receive remuneration for this. Indeed, Jesus himself spoke 'to' this when sending his disciples out:

'Do not get any gold or silver or copper to take with you in your belts – no bag for the journey or extra shirt or sandals or a staff, for the worker is worth his keep.' (Matthew 10:9–10)

Next we will look at ways for an evangelist to make a living.

Self-support: tent-making and other employment

After this, Paul left Athens and went to Corinth. There he met a Jew named Aquila, a native of Pontus, who had recently come from Italy with his wife Priscilla, because Claudius had ordered all Jews to leave Rome. Paul went to see them, and because he was a tentmaker as they were, he stayed and worked with them. Every Sabbath he reasoned in the synagogue, trying to persuade Jews and Greeks. (Acts 18:1–4)

From this passage we can see that Paul worked as a tentmaker during the week and preached the gospel of a Saturday.

For further reading on why Paul worked a day job, see the following: http://www.bible-bridge.com/pauls-income-four-reasons-why-paul-worked-day-job/

RESEARCH ACTIVITY

Expound various ways and means, with examples.

Gifts and offerings

* Do you stipulate an amount you require or do you just trust God to give you whatever you need?
* Do you take up love offerings for your ministry?

The elderly elder [of the church addresses this letter] to the beloved (esteemed) Gaius, whom I truly love. Beloved, I pray that you may prosper in every way and [that your body] may keep well, even as [I know] your soul keeps well and prospers. In fact, I greatly rejoiced when [some of] the brethren from time to time arrived and spoke [so highly] of the sincerity and fidelity of your life, as indeed you do live in the Truth [the whole Gospel presents]. I have no greater joy than this, to hear that my [spiritual] children are living their lives in the Truth. Beloved, it is a fine and faithful work that you are doing when you give any service to the [Christian] brethren, and [especially when they are] strangers. They have testified before the church of your love and friendship. You will do well to forward them on their journey [and you will please do so] in a way worthy of God's [service]. For these [travelling missionaries] have gone out for the Name's sake (for His sake) and are accepting nothing from the Gentiles (the heathen, the non-Israelites). So we ourselves ought to support such people [to welcome and provide for them], in order that we may be fellow workers in the Truth (the whole Gospel) and cooperate with its teachers. (3 John 1–8 AMP)

Monthly support from churches

- When you work as an evangelist for a number of churches on a regular basis, you can set up an agreed remuneration

Trust/charity

- Establish a trust/charity to raise funds
  Example: Billy Graham Evangelistic Association

Christian Stewardship

- Online giving portal

Resources

- Sell books, DVDs, downloads, subscriptions to podcasts

CHAPTER SIX

PERSONHOOD

We can all get caught up with 'titles' and 'positions' but remember: we are all fallible human beings at the end of the day. Evangelists have the same life challenges as everyone else and they are normal like everyone else; this means they, too, mess up. When asked who you are the answer should not be 'I am an evangelist'; it should be 'I am a son, daughter, father, mother,' etc. A job title does not define who a person is. We define the 'Who are you?' as Personhood.

Personhood is incredibly important, not just in the life of an evangelist but in the life of every Christian. The gift and calling of God can get you there but good character keeps you there! As previously stated we know that we all mess up from time to time, but as you can see in the media, people of prominent position get lambasted very quickly if they make a character mistake. We do have an enemy: the accuser of the brethren will jump on any mistake. God's grace is never ending, but people are different.

Personhood, however, is not just about self-discipline and guarding oneself against the enemy. It's all about life balance. Granted, Jesus did not promise an easy life, but you can enjoy the journey. After all, he came to give us life, and abundant life, and to turn our grief into joy!

So how do we get into 'good shape'?

Personhood more or less consists of the following elements:

1. Spiritual Life
2. Health
3. Family Life
4. Work Life
5. Finances
6. Friends / Social Life / Spare Time

These are the areas of life that can make or break us.

In fact, all of our needs and barriers to our calling are interwoven in the above.

Growing things change, and changing things grow. The key to progression is CHANGE. You cannot expect a different outcome by doing the same thing over and over. Perform the following self-audit giving yourself a score of between 1 (weak) to 10 (strong). You may find much that needs changing, but the key to ongoing success is honesty with yourself, and setting yourself small, achievable goals. All these smaller changes add up to a BIG change.

Small goals are achievable.

Achieving goals boosts your confidence.

Confidence keeps the momentum going!

Examples could be: reading your Bible every day, doing exercise for four hours a week, reconfiguring your household budget in order to save 10 per cent a week . . .

SELF AUDIT

Area
Score (1-10)
Goal (What? By when?)
! Remember: ? small ? achievable
Spiritual Life
Health
Family Life
Work Life
Finances
Friends/Social Life/Spare Time

'The Modesto Manifesto'

Billy Graham and his team resolved:

1. To never exaggerate attendance figures at their meetings.
    Guard against lying and deceit.

2. To take only a fixed salary from their organisation. Guard against financial thievery.

3. To never be alone with a woman other than their wife, mother, daughters. Guard against sexual sin. (Even guard against any potential appearance of it!)

4. To never criticise fellow members of the clergy. Guard against pride.

The 100 per cent non-negotiable requirement: holiness!

Make every effort to live in peace with all men and be holy; without holiness no one will see the Lord. (Hebrews 12:14)

What does 'being holy' mean?

Holiness is a description of God.

Each of the four living creatures had six wings and was covered with eyes all around, even under its wings. Day and night they never stop saying: 'Holy, holy, holy is the Lord God Almighty, who was, and is, and is to come.' (Revelation 4:8)

So we can say that being holy is being God-like.

How are we to be holy? How can we be like God when we are mere humans?

We have the perfect example: Jesus the God-man!

All we have to do is copy Jesus.

We know that we have come to know him if we keep his commands. Whoever says, 'I know him,' but does not do what he commands is a liar, and the truth is not in that person. But if anyone obeys his word, love for God is truly made complete in them. This is how we know we are in him: Whoever claims to live in him must live as Jesus did. (1 John 2:3–6)

A note on sin:

Holiness is synonymous with purity and sinlessness. God does not sin. But we do. How does that work then?

Well, it's purely a matter of decision making. Make the right decisions! There are three types of sin:

1.   Original sin: performed in the Garden of Eden by Adam and Eve. This sin is in all of us and there is nothing we can do about it. This is totally covered by the blood of Christ.

2.   Wilful sin: wilfully going against God's commands. Doing something wrong when you know it's wrong. This requires confession and repentance. When Jesus dealt with the woman at the well he told her to go 'and sin no more'. He did not say go 'and sin less'. The only unforgivable sin, the sin of unbelief and refusing to accept the sacrifice and salvation of the Son of God, falls into this category.

3.   Sin of ignorance: sinning when you do not know it is a sin. When this happens one usually has an uncomfortable feeling about what has happened. Conviction of the Holy Spirit. If this happens then confess it to the Lord and move on.

So, the only sin you have control over is wilful sin.

We are declared positionally righteous and holy by the blood of Jesus alone. We can, however, through repentance and the power of Almighty God working within us, walk in purity, the fruit of the Holy Spirit. Jesus is Lord and Saviour, Author and Finisher of our faith.

Humility

Oxford Dictionary: The quality of having a low estimate of one's own importance.

> *Now Moses was a very humble man, more humble than anyone else on the face of the earth.* (Numbers 12:3)

> *Take my yoke upon you and learn from me, for I am gentle and humble in heart, and you will find rest for your souls. For my yoke is easy and my burden is light.* (Matthew 11:29–30)

For most people, 'being humble' brings to mind a form of weakness. 'If someone practises humility, it means they're not a "go-getter" and don't care about performance or working hard. It's the weak one who is humble and is dependent on someone else.' If this is true, why do you suppose the Bible has so much to say about being humble? Maybe we've got it all wrong and the one who practises humility is actually the strong one?

Humble yourselves, therefore, under God's mighty hand, that he
may lift you up in due time. Cast all your anxiety on him
because he cares for you. (1 Peter 5:6–7)

God cares for us. He is mighty. He calls us to humble ourselves under him. Not because he is a controlling God that wants you to bow down to him because you are nothing, but rather because he wants to exalt us and care for us. As we humble ourselves, that is when we truly worship him in Spirit and in truth; when we're trusting him with what's going on in our lives and believing he is the provider instead of ourselves.

Stop putting everything on your shoulders

Are you busy? Are you weary? Are you taking on a lot of responsibilities? Are you working hard for your family? Are you trying to attend as many social events as possible? Are you trying to pay the bills as best as you can? Are you striving, just to 'get by'?

'Come to me, all you who are weary and burdened, and I will
give you rest. Take my yoke upon you and learn from me, for
I am gentle and humble in heart, and you will find rest for
your souls. For my yoke is easy and my burden is light.'
(Matthew 11:28–30)

Jesus doesn't seem to be describing a life full of anxiety and weariness in following him. He makes a point to state the exact opposite of how we can find rest in him! He is speaking to those that labour and are heavy laden.

Are we working too hard? Are we thinking way too much? Are we putting things on our shoulders that don't belong there? Are we forgetting what Jesus said and what he has done when we feel that it's 'all on us' to get things to happen? Most of the time, we're probably putting so much effort into all the wrong things.

In today's culture, we're told if you labour and are heavy laden then you are doing the right thing. You are sacrificing for your family and friends. You are pulling yourself up by your bootstraps and working hard to hopefully one day achieve paradise (retirement) where you get to do nothing as you live out the rest of your days. This is wrong. Don't let culture tell you that putting everything on your shoulders is wisdom. Trust Jesus when he tells you that his burden is light.

> *Rejoice in the Lord always. I will say it again: rejoice! Let your gentleness be evident to all. The Lord is near. Do not be anxious about anything, but in every situation, by prayer and petition, with thanksgiving, present your requests to God. And the peace of God, which transcends all understanding, will guard your hearts and your minds in Christ Jesus. Finally, brothers and sisters, whatever is true, whatever is noble, whatever is right, whatever is pure, whatever is lovely, whatever is admirable – if anything is excellent or praiseworthy – think about such things. Whatever you have learned or received or heard from me, or seen in me – put it into practice. And the God of peace will be with you.* (Philippians 4:4–9)

When we don't humble ourselves, we are really saying that we don't trust God. There are times as a follower of Christ when we forget God's character or doubt him. We're told in Scripture to think on the things of God, to meditate on anything worthy of praise.

These things that are true, honourable, just, pure, lovely, commendable, or excellent are all praiseworthy because God is all these things. You'll never find an area of the Bible that contradicts God's character, and that should encourage us in those moments of doubt.

God gave his one and only son for us. This tells us a lot about his character. That doesn't sound like a God who is a tyrant and just demands power all the time. It doesn't match up to a God that doesn't care about us. He knew that we could only come to him through his son who had to suffer and die before rising again. With that perfect knowledge, which only God can have, he followed through and sacrificed his son for us. Not only does that tell us everything we need to know about God's character, that shows us just how much he loves us.

Jesus is our ultimate example of humility. Out of obedience to his Father, he humbled himself all the way to the point of death on the cross.

> *And being found in appearance as a man, he humbled himself by becoming obedient to death – even death on a cross!* (Philippians 2:8–11)

Therefore God exalted him to the highest place and gave him the name that is above every name, that at the name of Jesus every knee should bow, in heaven and on earth and under the earth, and every tongue acknowledge that Jesus Christ is Lord, to the glory of God the Father.

If Jesus practised humility himself, then why would we think we don't need to? Why would we consider this to be weakness? Even he was dependent on his Father and this was a good thing; in fact, the best thing. It was a God glorifying thing in every way. We couldn't even have a relationship with God if it wasn't for what Jesus did for us in the first place. We had to humble ourselves to trust that Jesus is King and to ask him to be our Lord and Saviour. This is no different today whether you've been a believer for a week or 50 years.

We still need him in everything we do. We still need the Holy Spirit to guide us and give us wisdom in all matters. We still need help to practise things that are honourable, pure, lovely, commendable, or anything praiseworthy. We are still not capable of doing anything on our own and will never be. As soon as we begin to live in a way where we are no longer dependent on God to do everything for us, we are forgetting our first love and proclaiming what Christ did for us was not enough.

As a follower of Christ, no matter what circumstance you find yourself in, you can give it to him. This is because God's Word is true. What Jesus did was enough. And you have the Holy Spirit and can trust him to lead and guide you. Humble yourself and pray to God, truly casting your anxieties on Him and trust that he does indeed care for you.

CHAPTER SEVEN

SHARING THE MESSAGE

The message of the evangelist in simple: KISS! (Keep It Simple, Sanctified!) God loves you: Jesus died for you. Turn from your sin (missing the mark), and turn to the finished work of Jesus on the cross for forgiveness of your sins. Bringing people to assurance of Salvation is imperative and here's where reliance on the work and person of the Holy Spirit is also essential.

> *For God so loved the world that he gave his one and only Son, that whoever believes in him shall not perish but have eternal life.* (John 3:16)

> *And I will ask the Father, and he will give you another advocate to help you and be with you forever.* (John 14:16)

> *But you will receive power when the Holy Spirit comes on you; and you will be my witnesses in Jerusalem, and in all Judea and Samaria, and to the ends of the earth.* (Acts 1:8)

Etiquette and Ethical Protocol

- Lines of communication
- Relationships
- Dos and don'ts

> *So Christ himself gave the apostles, the prophets, the evangelists, the pastors and teachers, to equip his people for works of service, so that the body of Christ may be built up until we all reach unity in the faith and in the knowledge of the Son of God and become mature, attaining to the whole measure of the fullness of Christ.* (Ephesians 4:11–13)

Build and keep a good relationship with those with other ascension gift ministries, as mentioned above. This is essential! Also, be careful when building relationships with congregation members, to respect the authority and role of the pastors and their teams: this will help prevent things getting messy.

Don't play on slippery slopes, that's how better people than you and I have fallen! As with the Billy Graham Modesto Manifesto, no time alone with anyone of the opposite sex outside of family.

What is the message?

- The gospel!

- What is the gospel? The good news of salvation through Jesus Christ!

- What is the call to salvation? It is surrendering your life to Christ: Giving your will for your life over to God's will.

    Therefore, I urge you, brothers and sisters, in view of God's mercy, to offer your bodies as a living sacrifice, holy and pleasing to God – this is your true and proper worship. Do not conform to the pattern of this world, but be transformed by the renewing of your mind. Then you will be able to test and approve what God's will is – his good, pleasing and perfect will. (Romans 12:1–2)

We must share a message of complete surrender at the first opportunity, surrendering our lives to God's salvation plan for our lives. This is good news! God's redemptive plan is a lot better than any we have.

How to convey the message

The Art of Storytelling

The gift of the evangelist often carries the art of storytelling. Many of the greats – D.L. Moody, George Whitfield, and our modern-day friend J.John – use storytelling to give powerful illustrations and anecdotes. Why not study and sharpen these gifts and communication skills that allow us to engage with unbelievers in a powerful and relevant way, without losing the potency of the gospel, the Spirit and the Word of God.

Altar Calls

These can be many and varied. Reflect on the first 'altar call' given after Jesus' ascension:

> *When the people heard this, they were cut to the heart and said to Peter and the other apostles, 'Brothers, what shall we do?' Peter replied, 'Repent and be baptised, every one of you, in the name of Jesus Christ for the forgiveness of your sins. And you will receive the gift of the Holy Spirit. The promise is for you and your children and for all who are far off – for all whom the Lord our God will call.' With many other words he warned them; and he pleaded with them, 'Save yourselves from this corrupt generation.' Those who accepted his message were baptised, and about three thousand were added to their number that day.* (Acts 2:37–41)

As Peter in Acts 2:1–36 laid out the sinfulness of man, so, too, Jonathan Edwards (a great awakening revivalist) preached of sinners in the hands of an angry God! However, the wrath of God is then *fully satisfied* in the finished work of Jesus on the cross!

Inviting Jesus into your heart and life:

1. There is a heaven to gain! (Good news to rejoice in!)
2. There is a hell to shun. (Reality to be aware of.)
3. There is a need: to turn from our sin. (Meaning of sin = missing the mark.)
4. There is a decision to be made. (To follow Jesus, take up our cross daily, die to self, i.e. anything where my will is in conflict with God's will, Word, Spirit.)

Mobilising: equipping the saints/congregants into works of service

Ephesians 4:11–13 again!
Training the people, teaching the people (the people = the Church = the Body of Christ):

- Who they are in Christ.
- What they have in Christ (i.e. ALL we need for life and godliness).

And then, how to share the good news out of a spiritual overflow. (We ALL have an anointing and are commissioned to win the lost, not just the evangelist.)

The Hard Facts

Fact 1. Not many win people to Christ or even share their faith.
Fact 2. Not many want to or desire to.
Fact 3. Not many find it easy to build friendships with non-believers.

We *have to* address the above. How can we do this?

1. **Stay on fire ourselves and be practitioners.** D.L. Moody sought to win at least one person daily to Christ. Yes, this will take continued prayer, study and action! Keeping this at the forefront of our hearts, minds and actions. Be intentional about soul winning.

2. **Then we can authentically equip others** to do the same. The power is in the gospel, not us. We are the messengers.

Impartation

Impartation is being around bigger ministries than ourselves, the smearing, the mentorship from another. The laying on of hands, stirring up the gift that is in you.

> *For this reason I remind you to fan into flame the gift of God, which is in you through the laying on of my hands.*
> (2 Timothy 1:6)

The apostle Paul writes to his young protégé Timothy, encouraging him to do the work of an evangelist, to fan his gift into flame, to stay on fire!

Follow up/next steps discipleship

- Use resources: DVDs, CDs, online resources, booklets (both your own work and that of others)
- Lock into the local church, work with the local church

- Encourage participation in discipleship courses and developing a lifestyle that is accountable to and consistent with the Word of God

Raising Evangelists

Seek to mentor and help others with the same heart and call of the evangelist. Reach up and reach down. Help in lifting them up and getting them established. We are all on that journey, and we all need help along the way.

Barriers

What issues have you faced in the area of evangelism?

Lacking finance/provision?

We need to overcome this; each for their own ministry and to help others in their ministries.

1. Believe God: he is our source.
2. Tap into Christian stewardship, sowing and reaping, raising partners, major donors, targeted fundraising, multiple income streams, church support, gifts and offerings; knowing full well that where God guides, he provides; where he leads, he feeds! These are not just clichés but powerful, fundamental truths.

Lacking opportunities?

1. Pray.
2. Find a way to promote and market your ministry.
3. Network! Keep building relationships, and make use of the ones you already have!
4. Ask for recommendations.
5. Go! Even whilst we are praying and waiting for the above, the command is to go now! Start with what you have. We can tell ourselves and the devil, we will win souls one-on-one whilst we are waiting! And because you've gone after and valued the souls that nobody else wants, you'll get the souls that everybody wants! We have seen this.

Lacking credibility?

1. Stay planted in the local church.

2. Maintain good friendships.

3. Stay planted in your close and *affirming family*. (Be warned: not all will affirm the call of God on your life.)

4. Ask for references from credible ministries and friends.

5. Stay true to the Word of God. Live it!

6. Live a holy and humble life; be quick to repent and keep close accounts with God and friends.

Experiencing loneliness?

This goes with the territory. It can be very lonely at times. That's why it's important, and I emphasise again, stay in church, stay close to God and the comfort of the Holy Spirit. Time alone with God in study and prayer is essential.

Experiencing inconsistency?

Keep doing the right things, over and over and over again!

Needs

- Coaching/affirmation: get friendly and stay close to those who have gone before you.

- Anointing: stay under the anointing – the empowerment of God to do the task. Never put your trust or confidence in your own strength or ability.

- DSPs (divine strategic partnerships): Ask! God will give you these. In Luke 5, Peter needed friends to bring in the largest catch ever! So do we! Signal to friends in other boats – churches, ministries, callings, supporters. Again, reach up and down. Pray, look, knock and know that Jesus – who is the same yesterday, today and forever (Hebrews 13:8) – still provides.

CHAPTER EIGHT

ONE-ON-ONE EVANGELISM

Tips on where to start with one-on-one evangelism . . .

So, everybody's different right? No two people speak exactly the same
way, look the same, smell the same, and dress the same. One thing that
is common to many Christians I've met, however, is a difficulty when it
comes to sharing their faith. I'm not sure it was meant to be that way. I've
mentioned before that when we look at the early church in the book of
Acts, they went out in the boldness and power of the Holy Spirit and not
a lot of fear! For a lot of people today, fear seems to be the major issue
– being afraid of what others may think or may say. Well here are five
things that hopefully will be a starting point to help you overcome those
fears if you struggle to share your faith . . .

1. Pray

This is obviously not rocket science but as someone (John Wesley,
I think?) said, 'Before we talk to the people about God, we need to talk
to God about the people!' We can never be effective in our witnessing
and evangelism if we don't pray.

2. Rely on the Holy Spirit

German evangelist Reinhard Bonnke says, 'The Holy Spirit is the master
evangelist.' A whole number of blogs could be written on this one subject,
but the key thing for us to realise is that it is not down to us to save the
world – Jesus is the Saviour and the Holy Spirit brings conversion (John
16:7–12). Our job is to share the gospel and we do that best when we rely
on the Holy Spirit to prompt us, empower us and equip us with the
words to say!

3.   Share your story

So many people say 'I'm not called to be an evangelist'. Well maybe not, but we are all called to be witnesses (Acts 1:7–9). That means telling our story of how Jesus changed our lives. We may not feel we have the gifting or training of an evangelist (yet!) but we do have our own experience of knowing Jesus. Telling your story is a great place to start when it comes to evangelism!

4.   Don't feel guilty

As I've mentioned, so many people feel guilty about the fact that they have not been sharing their faith. They want to do more, they try to do more, but it just doesn't seem to happen. The enemy is very good at making us feel guilty. One word of advice: relax. Yes, the gospel is urgent and we need to get on with the job of telling people, but sometimes we can run ahead of ourselves and we try to do things in our own strength instead of taking the time to pray and trust the Holy Spirit! Having said that, I've had times I've felt prompted by the Holy Spirit to say something to someone and have just shrugged it off. If we miss an opportunity we just have to repent and ask the Lord to open up another one, and try to be ready when that one comes along!

5.   Don't be afraid to say 'I don't know'

Quite often we can be held back from witnessing because we feel inadequate. We don't feel we have enough knowledge. We're worried someone might ask us a difficult question and we won't know how to answer it. There are two ways to deal with this problem. The first is to have the courage to say 'I don't know' – but then we need to follow that with 'but I'll try to find out'. Maybe meet the person with your pastor or find someone else who will help you answer the question. (One thing we do need to try to discern is if the question is genuine or not.) The second way to help with this issue is for us to know the Bible as best we can, read it regularly and to commit to memory certain Bible verses that we feel will be helpful to us in our witnessing. It's amazing how the Holy Spirit can bring a verse back to our minds at just the right time!

Steve Mullins (Dry Bones Trust)

www.drybonestrust.org

Training and equipping the local church: 5 sessions over a weekend with a local church

1. It's Time to Flourish
2. It's All Working Out
3. Don't Deny the Power
4. Beyond the Open Door
5. Divine Strategic Partnership

The simplest tool you'll ever use . . .

The4points

One of the ways you can start a conversation with someone is to give them one of the hand-out cards. You'll see on this card a heart, a multiplication sign, a cross (as in the cross of Christ), then a question mark. There you go. So really, it's the gospel made simple. I say, can the simple gospel message really change people's lives today? Can it? Are you sure? Are you really sure? Absolutely!

A simple gospel message can still change people's lives today.

First point: God loves me.
Second point: I have sinned.
Third point: Jesus died for me.
Fourth point: I need to decide to live for God.

And then you can see the prayer at the end. I mean, how simple can that be?

For examples of one-on-one evangelism conversations and further explanation of the4points, please see Appendix 1.

CHAPTER NINE

THE CHURCH:
STAYING PLANTED IN THE FAMILY

The righteous will flourish like a palm tree, they will grow like a cedar of Lebanon; planted in the house of the LORD, they will flourish in the courts of our God. They will still bear fruit in old age, they will stay fresh and green. (Psalm 92:12–14)

Prerequisites always bring promises!

1. We will flourish.
2. We will bear fruit.
3. We will stay fresh.

Staying planted in your local church is absolutely essential and non-negotiable for personal health, scriptural obedience and credibility. This is one of the things (if not the main thing!) that has kept me – and many others – 'on the straight and narrow' over the years. A coal burns much brighter when with other coals. The church is God's family, where we are cared for, mobilised, loved, taught and enjoy fun, friendship and food. It's what Christ is committed to building and the gates of hell will not prevail against it! No church is perfect; if you find a 'perfect' one don't join that or you'll make it imperfect! (Joke!) When people are looking for the perfect church, they are always disappointed because it doesn't exist! Not yet, anyway.

Guidelines on staying planted:

1. Remember, your church is home.
2. Try to attend your home church at least once a month.
3. Build and maintain good relationships, especially with the leader(s).
4. Give.

5. Receive.

6. Be an active part of your church.

7. Speak well of your church, leaders, fellow worshippers. Be an encourager!

RECOMMENDED READING

Chasing the Dragon (Jackie Pullinger)
The Cross and the Switchblade (David Wilkerson)
Living a Life of Fire (Reinhard Bonnke)
Biographies of: George Whitefield, D.L. Moody, Hudson Taylor

APPENDIX 1:

TRANSCRIPT OF TRAINING SESSION – THE4POINTS

Welcome to the first Evangelist Academy that we're doing in this manner. I feel very honoured and very excited! This is very key, what we're doing today; it's so important, it's so the heart of God, it's so the will of God, so with us, for us, behind us, it's the heart of the Christian faith. We've got the great commandment: 'Love one another'; and then we've got the great commission: 'Go, seek the lost, make disciples of all nations' – for you are disciples! So we're going to share about a bit. We're going to demystify and take away some fear factors around one-on-one evangelism, because really, God doesn't tell us to do anything that isn't out of our league or zone. 'Oh well, I'm not an evangelist,' you say. Well, you might not be, but I am, and the gift of the evangelist is to train you and to mobilise you and to impart into you, *so you can do the work* of the evangelist. Paul said that to Timothy, didn't he? 2 Timothy 3:5 says, 'Having a form of godliness but denying its power. Have nothing to do with such people.' The answer to 2 Timothy 3:5 is actually 2 Timothy 4:5 – 'But you, keep your head in all situations, endure hardship, do the work of an evangelist, discharge all the duties of your ministry.' He says that to the pastors, and we know pastors have got the heart for evangelism!

So that's just a bit of an introduction. I'm going to read a couple of scriptures and then we'll do some training, some praying, and then we're going to go out in teams, and meet back here afterwards. Let's just pray before we start.

> *Lord Jesus, we thank you that your heart is to come and seek, and save that which was lost. Thank you that that's why you came, Lord, to seek and save those that are lost, to destroy the works of the enemy, and you came that we might have life, and have it more abundantly. Lord, we lift this Evangelist Academy session to you, we ask for your anointing on your word, Lord,*

and on this training. We pray for impartation and empowerment, and we pray for the labourers, Lord, that are here today, and for anointing as we go – for we know that the harvest is ripe, the fields are ripened to harvest! We pray that hearts will be open and receptive, Lord. As we go, we pray for your protection, we pray for your joy, your spirit of fun and adventure, Lord. Anoint everybody here, Lord, and anybody who listens to this within the sound of my voice, or from reading these words, with the anointing of evangelism, Lord, the gift of the evangelist released and stood up for you – that people may be one for you, in the name of Jesus. And everybody said? 'Amen.'

If you've got your Bibles with you, turn to Mark 16:15–17.

And then he told them, 'Go into all the world and preach the good news to everyone. Anyone who believes and is baptised will be saved, but anyone who refuses to believe will be condemned. These miraculous signs will accompany those who believe.'

Jesus is telling us to go and preach the gospel – the good news. Those who believe and receive will be saved; those who don't are damned already. That's a fact! Jill pulled a face then, questioning 'damned'. Well it's true, they are, like we were once damned, but we're not going to damn people, we're going to share the good news, and I'll talk more about that later. And the great thing about Jesus is, everything he asks us to do, he goes with us and he empowers us to do. Isn't that great? So we're really, really, fulfilling the great commission here today. We're fulfilling God's plan, and the prayer of Jesus, so all heaven is behind us, all heaven is literally on our side today. So be encouraged! There are people following us all around the UK and all around the world, and they're praying for us this morning. Isn't that great!

So, we're doing what Jesus wants us to do. Do you remember the wristbands? 'What would Jesus do?' Well, this is exactly what he would do, and did. You know what I mean? People used to make it all super-spiritual didn't they, 'What would Jesus do?' Jesus would do this, or do that. Well actually, he came to seek and save the lost, destroy the works of the enemy, and he came that we might have life and have it at its fullness. So that's good, isn't it? Amen forevermore!

Onto our next scripture, Luke 10:2 – and I'm only reading these two scriptures – why make it complicated?

'Then he said to them, "The harvest is plentiful, but the workers are few. Ask the Lord of the harvest, therefore, to send out workers into his harvest field."'

So we're fulfilling the prayer of Jesus, right here, right now, and the prayer of the early disciples. We, today, in this room, and those listening to the recording, or reading about it, are fulfilling the prayer of Jesus, fulfilling the great commission, and that really excites me. What is God's will for my life? This, this is it. If we can just keep this heart, and keep this spirit. . . I like John Wesley, who said this, 'God rewards those who go after souls.' He does. I've always been a soul winner, and God has always rewarded me. What scripture? Hebrews 11:6 says that we must first believe that God exists when we come to him, and secondly we must believe that he's a rewarder of those who diligently seek him. At no time can we see God more, than when we are diligently seeking him for the souls of men and women, boys and girls. Amen.

So, get ready for God openly rewarding you, and continuing to reward you as you continue to be a soul winner! Amen. Praise God! So I'm just going to share a little now about how we're going to do this soul winning. As I'm doing that, Jill is going to give everybody a free gift. Anybody like a free gift? Yes, of course – everyone likes a free gift! While that's happening, I'll just talk you through the soul-winning script which we're going to use today.

The4points

It's a four-point soul-winning script, and I really like these. I've spoken to Dave Sharples, who is the director of this Christian ministry. Since 1993 he's been a youth worker in Liverpool; he actually got an MBE! He worked with young people in Toxteth, which is like a ghetto, all the riots were in Toxteth – you might remember that. He tried to make the church more accessible and relevant to local families by communicating the gospel in a simple and memorable way. In 1995 he and his wife visited Metro Ministries in New York and were really inspired by the work of Bill Wilson – especially how he used a really simple way to communicate the essence of the gospel. It's called 'the four most important things in the world!' and is a mixture of the wordless gospel Spurgeon created way back in 1866 to explain the gospel to inner-city orphans in London, and the four spiritual laws tract written by Bill Bright in 1952. Anyway, Dave and the team started teaching the four most important things every week but changed the name to 'the4points' to make it simpler. Then in 2005 Dave and his friend Nick Gillard came up with this graphic logo based on the4points. They wanted to create a cryptic and intriguing mathematical equation that would spark conversations and help people to share their faith. They realised they had inadvertently created a tool for international evangelism that broke both the literacy and language barriers, which is amazing! They've got wristbands as well as the fold-out tracts, and the tracts can even be personalised on the back panel, to help with follow up, and are available in over twenty languages.

So look at the rich heritage we're tapping into here; it's great, isn't it? 'The Four Spiritual Laws' written by Bill Bright in 1952 and inspired by Spurgeon in the 1800s, then Bill Wilson with 'the four most important things', and now my friend Dave Sharples with the4points which I'm just going to talk you through now. In fact, we need to give everybody one of these; you can just take one and pass them round. It's the four points. Everybody say 'four points'. It's not a four-point sermon, it's just four points. It's not four points and a poem, it's just simply four points.

On the back it explains it more; I'll go through it. The4points is a very simple overview of the Bible. The first thing you need to know is that God is crazy about you, and it is unconditional. There is nothing you can do that will make God love you any more, or any less, than he already does right now. There is nothing God wants more than to love and be loved by humans. **First point.**

The second point: I have sinned. Sadly, we have been separated from God's love by something the Bible calls sin. Simply put, sin is when we do something to please ourselves rather than God. We sin when we ignore God, break his laws and basically do something our own way that is contrary to God's way. Sin destroys relationships with friends, with family and with God. The Bible says that sin, ultimately, brings death. That's a great point, a really, really good point to share with people, and I'll explain more on this later.

So then, the wages of sin is death, but the gift of God is eternal life. We all want a free gift, don't we? Yes? We all want a free gift. You all wanted a free gift today, and that leads us to 'Jesus died for me'. **The third point** is probably one of the most well-known facts in the history of mankind, but is often misunderstood. The key is to realise that the penalty for sin is death. We've all sinned, and we all deserve to die, but God, who is full of mercy, loves you so much that he sent Jesus to die in your place. Jesus died so that we can have eternal life. It's a free gift.

Fourth point: I need to decide to live for God. Not only did Jesus die for our sin, but three days later he rose from the dead! Through his death and resurrection, Jesus now made a way for us to have a relationship with God. All you need to do is to accept that you've sinned, ask for God's forgiveness, and then decide to live the rest of your life for him. The choice is yours.

Then there's a prayer on the back. If you turn it over, you can see the four steps here, the four points: God loves me. I have sinned. Jesus died for me. I need to decide to live for God. And it looks really cool, doesn't it? Don't you think? I think it looks great; young people would like something like this. It looks like emoticon kind of speak, looks great, is really well produced. So this in itself would be a good gift, but we're going to do more than that because a lot of people just go and give tracks out and people don't really know why. But we're going to talk people through this and I'll explain to you how to do it and train you and help you to do it. But let's practise on one another before we go out.

And just while we're talking about this, what's really good about this method is it totally depersonalises it, i.e. it's really not dependent on you. You can point people to the script which is pointing people to the plan of redemption, the plan of salvation. I'll talk more about that, but it's really about keeping it simple, the KISS Principle: Keep It Simple Sanctified. Amen. So you've all been sanctified and we can keep it simple and I just want to give a couple of testimonies of how we have done this, Jill and I. You know, I could say I don't really need a script, because I don't; I do this all the time – my wife will tell you – everywhere I go I do it, I lead people to Christ. But for us all, now, this is a great tool for us all to use and not just today, but it will train you and equip you for the rest of your life. Just imagine this, right: we get to heaven and we're standing in front of Jesus and it's all going to be great, which it is, but there's a moment at the judgement seat of Christ, where we will all stand before Christ and be judged for everything we have done, or not done. Yes, we've been redeemed; yes, we've been forgiven. But we're going to be in the eternity of eternities and can you imagine getting to heaven and never actually leading anyone to Christ or bringing anyone with you or behind you? It's OK, you'll get in, but imagine the great rejoicing when people come to you and say, 'I'm so thankful that you shared the gospel with me. I'm so glad.' We're literally going to be snatching people from hell because there is a hell to shun and a heaven to gain. That's the good news that we're sharing.

So the first testimony that comes to mind was when we were in London. We were in five days of revival meetings at the O2 in London, just like we've been in here, meeting in here, getting touched by the power of God, getting refreshed, getting all this, but all that is so we can share the gospel. That's what it's all about; otherwise it's a total waste of time, a social club, a 'bless me' club. But we're blessed so we can go! So, Jill and I were at the O2 and we went out for lunch or a drink, and we were exploring around the O2 and we ended up in a VIP airport lounge, with stewardesses and stewards welcoming you. It was all very James Bond, very high tech and looked great, very cool, just opened. I love stuff like that. So we go in and they are showing us round and we're talking to the guy, who was very effeminate (I'm just setting the scene) and he's showing us this lounge and that lounge, and 'Would you like a drink?' So we sit down, are talking, he's telling us who he is and what he does and then he says to me, 'And what do you do?'

(Good question, isn't it? I said, 'Well, I'm glad you asked.' I said I'm like a modern-day missionary, that's what I am. That's a good way of putting it, isn't it? That's what you are, right now. And that's good, because it leads people to ask, 'What is a modern-day missionary?')

He wants to know more . . . 'Well, I go round the world and I tell people "God loves them, Jesus died for them and he's got a plan for their life."'

'Really, yeah, great, that's good. Well, actually, I used to go to church, been to church,' – don't get into the church thing with people; there's no need to do it, you'll just be there debating, arguing all day.

'Oh great, OK. Has anybody ever told you God loves you, Jesus died for you, and he's got a plan for your life?'

'Well, not really.'

'Well he does and he has. Did you know the wages of sin is death but the gift of God is eternal life?'

He does all the 'I'm a good guy, I've done good, I've done all this and that.'

'Oh, that's good. Did you know the Bible says all of us have fallen short of the glory of God?'

And it's like this: I've told him 'God loves me'. Now I'm moving onto 'I have sinned. You have sinned. Do you know you have sinned? We've all sinned, right, but Jesus died for you. The gift of God is eternal life, to all those who receive.' Now the next one: 'I need to decide to live for God.' So the gift of God is eternal life, and we all want a free gift, don't we? I've been saying that time and time again – it's a good point! So what do I do straight away then? I ask, 'Would you mind if I pray with you and for you?' Most times, nine times out of ten, people say, 'No I don't mind. Yes, please pray for me,' and this is what I do. You've got a script here, so you can actually read and pray the script over them. Or you can change it. *Dear God, thank you that you love [Kevin / Steve / whatever their name is]. That you have a good plan and purpose for his life.'* And just pray blessing over them. That's what I did. *'Bless him, bless his family, give him a great life, empower him, pray good stuff and I pray that he'll accept you quickly. Amen.'*

'Would you like to accept Christ right now?' (It's what I said to him – would you like to? It's like closing the deal if you're in sales. Calling people to Christ. You've already prayed with him and for him, prayed good prayers.) 'Would you like to accept the free gift of salvation right now?'

'Yes.'

'Well OK, pray with me as I pray this prayer . . .

Dear Lord Jesus, come into my life, forgive me of my sin.' (Now all the stuff's on here you can pray.)

'Sorry for ignoring you and doing things my way. I realise now that my sin has hurt you and the people around me, and for this I'm truly sorry. Thank you, Jesus, that you gave your life for me and took the punishment for my sins. Please forgive me and help me now by the power of your Holy Spirit as I decide to live for you. Amen.'

Amen! Praise God! And then you can give them that. Now, I did that and the guy turned to me and said, 'Wow, can you feel that?!'

I said, 'Yes, I can feel that. I do feel that, I feel that all the time, everywhere I go.' I said, 'Not everyone feels it, but I'm so pleased you felt it.'

But he felt the anointing because we'd been saturated in meetings like you've been and something happens to you, and it'll never leave you. You receive an impartation and we'll pray that over you today before we go. But can you see how simple that is? Friends of ours take their children on the streets soul winning. Obviously they are with their parents and other trusted adults, but they go and all they are doing is using the script. This soul winning script. Amen!

Jill's going to tell you about another time we did that with somebody, led them to Christ.

[Jill] I probably had more input in the last example than this one. Actually the guy at the O2 was Catholic, so we asked him, 'If you were to die tonight, do you know where you would go?' He said, 'Oh, yes. I'd go to heaven because I'm a good boy and I've not done anything wrong.' And quite often people will say that: 'I'm a good person, I haven't done anything wrong.' I digress.

So, we were in Florida, in October and it was quite late, probably about one o'clock in the morning, and we were working our way back to our accommodation, when we stopped. We were trying to find somewhere to eat and we found this place called IHOP, International House of Pancakes (not International House of Prayer!), so in we went for something to eat and we were eating and chatting to the lady serving us. Very upbeat, very nice lady, and at the end this young lady had gone outside and we were getting ready to go and were heading towards the car and Terry thanks the young lady for serving us.

'Oh, why are you guys over here?'

'We're actually at a ministers' and leaders' conference.'

'Oh right,' and it turned out her sister was a Christian. Terry said, 'Do you know that God loves you and that Jesus died for you and has got a plan for your life?' I think at that point she just burst into tears, and said, 'Ahhh, you know, my sister is a Christian.' And I think she'd been going through quite a bad time, I think she'd been quite sick. Yes, she'd lost her husband, only a very young woman, maybe 30, and she was in absolutely streams of tears and Terry said, 'Well, God has obviously sent us here,' because nowhere else was open, everywhere else had just closed, just this one restaurant was open. 'God sent us to this place, by divine appointment so that we can pray with you.' And she accepted Christ and we actually saw her on another evening that week as well, and she was completely different. Although she was upbeat both times, you could see her face was different this time. You know, she didn't have that heaviness, didn't have that weight upon her.

Again, I think Terry probably just took her hand. I was there as well, so probably not a good idea for women to grab guy's hands or vice versa if they are not with other people – you know, make sure there is somebody with you. Just to be careful – you never know. Anyway, Terry prayed in Jesus's name and again she felt the presence of the Holy Spirit. I think often in church we don't realise how amazing this is, because we become familiar and we become used to the presence of God. Like the guy at the O2, he was like 'Can you feel that? Can you feel that?!' because he had never before felt the presence of God. So often we can think, 'I'm not going to say anything to this person, they are going to think I'm crazy.' But when we do, the Holy Spirit comes and does something amazing with that person. We just speak boldly, you know, with love. We're not there to beat people over the head, we're there to share the love of God and see people come to Christ.

My goodness, we were just thinking about this the other night – digressing slightly here – but there's a film called *Zoolander*, I think there's a second one coming out. Some people may never have heard of this film – it's a bit crazy – but there's a person in that by the name of David Bowie. I'm sure you've all heard of David Bowie, and that film was shot 15 years ago and you think, 'He looks great in this movie, 15 years ago,' but he just died this year. Now 15 years: you think, is it that long since that film's been made? Now it doesn't seem that long (although it was) but we're all getting older, every single one of us and nobody knows how long we're going to be on this earth. We don't know do we, and we've had many times when we've been in a place and shared the gospel with someone and we don't know if today is this person's last day on earth or if they will live to a ripe old age. We don't know. So we just pray that God guides our steps today. We're not here to beat people, to make them become Christians. This is *good news,* isn't it? Good news, the gospel. There's plenty of rubbish out there on the television. If people are watching EastEnders, they are going to get an East End life, aren't they? Rubbish in, rubbish out. So we want to give people good news.

[Terry] Isn't that good testimony, eh? It was amazing! And do you know the thing was, we'd eaten in IHOP and then we were going back to the car, and then I saw the lady having a smoke and I said, 'I've just got to go. I've got to go back.' And I went back to her and that's when I say, 'Has anybody told you that God loves you and Jesus died for you; that he's got a plan for your life?' So that's the tack we're going to be using today. We're going to be using the script and 'Has anybody ever told you God loves you, Jesus died for you and has a plan for your life?' That's how we start. Whether the answer is 'No' or 'Yes', ask, 'Can I just talk you through this?' That's how we do it. 'Has anybody told you God loves you? The Bible says we've all sinned, Jesus has died for you, and would you like to decide whether or not you want to live for God?' It's that simple; really that simple. Keep taking them back to the script if they try and take you away, about church or this or that. Take them back to the script. Would you mind if I pray with you and for you? Most people will say, 'OK, pray for me,' so you pray. *'Dear Lord, just bless [Kevin / Harry / Louise], bless them, bless their family, give them a long life, and satisfy them.'* I just pray some scriptural stuff and then *'I pray they will receive you quickly. Amen.'*

Well if they say that – because, it's interesting, it's a good question, and it's a good point because people do say that – 'Will you pray for me?' – I always say yes and just start praying for them. If they ask you to pray for them, pray for them. This is where we need to be on the front foot, right? Of course, we go in love, but be on the front foot. I mean people say that to me, 'Will you please pray for me?' so I say, 'Yes, let's just bow your head right now.' Do you know what I mean? Because otherwise it's just religious, it's rubbish.

If they are going somewhere, ask if you can walk with them and pray with them. Do that, OK? That's what we do. I've known people get led to Christ while just walking down the street with them to the Tube or whatever. Seriously. So it's like eliminating 'excusia' and using 'exousia' – which is 'delegated empowerment' or 'authority and conferred influential power' and we're going step out in that power. Acts 1:8 says, 'But you will receive power when the Holy Spirit comes on you; and you will be my witnesses' . . . in Thamesmead, in Woolwich, in south London, wherever! The uttermost parts of the earth. We're actually at the uttermost part of the earth today!

You can use the same principle with your family, of course! It's a good principle. I've led my mum to the Lord, I've led two sisters to the Lord. I'm still going for my two brothers! But, this is a great tool because it depersonalises it from you, because they know you, they know how to navigate and wrestle you, like wrestling a bear. And it might be like that today for some of you, if you are thinking, 'Oh well I've tried that, done that,' whatever, fighting fear and all that, but you'll get an anointing from God and you can go and do it. And this is a proven tool, you know what I mean? So just keep taking them back to the script. We're going to practise on one another in a short while.

Of course, if you have some cards for the local church you can give them out, and anybody who does accept Christ and you pray with them, give them a card to the church, or invite them to church if you like. If you are visiting an area and don't know of a specific local church, the best guidance to give people who are looking to find a church is to tell them to look for one that is Christ-centred and Bible-based.

But while the church is immensely important, try for this moment in time, to forget church. Seriously, in this moment, we're winning souls, and let me tell you something before we start practising on each other. I was on the back streets of Manchester, I was addicted to drugs, was a drug dealer, a criminal. People would keep away from me; I was quite dangerous. I thought I ran the estate, like one of the estates round here, and we'd sit in front of the shops, me and my guys, friends, thinking we run things. And this guy used to come and say, 'God loves you, Jesus died for you and he's got a plan for your life.' He'd look me in the eye with boldness and courage. He came to me and told me that. Everybody else tried to take the mickey out of him and I said, 'No, listen. I want to listen to this guy.' So somebody came and told me about Jesus. He didn't mention church, no church at all. Shortly afterwards, I went to his house. He led me to Christ:

'God loves you, Jesus died for you and has a plan for your life. Do you want to turn from your sin? Do you want to receive Christ as your Saviour?'

'Yes I do.' I got down on my knees and prayed the prayer, right then and there.

Of course, he followed me up, but I didn't particularly feel like I needed to be followed up. The Holy Spirit followed me up, do you know what I'm saying? What does the Bible say? It doesn't say go and 'just' invite them to church. Amen. Is that right? You see this is simple: it says go and preach the gospel. That's all it says to do, do you know what I mean?

So today we're fulfilling the great commission. We're going to go and share the good news and we're going to lead people to Christ. Amen. So all I'm doing is cutting through, like, preconditioning and training for most people who haven't led zip to Christ – do you know what I mean? Haven't led anybody to Christ. They just haven't done it and they are full of excusia, and they are full of religion and they are full of dead men's bones. But I tell you something: when you go and share the good news, I can feel the anointing right now, because when you share the good news, it does you more good than them! Think about it! 'Wow, God loves me, Jesus died for me, he's got a plan for my life, wow.' You know what I mean? Come on, it's great isn't it? So you're reaffirming the gospel in your own life and Acts 1:8 – 'and you shall be witnesses when this power comes upon you'. When you witness to the power of God, the power comes. I'm like this all the time. The gospel is the power of God unto salvation. First to them who believe. Amen. So if it's first to them who believe, that's you who believe, that's me. That's the scripture, isn't it?

The gospel is the power of God unto salvation. Wholeness, fullness, *sozo*, peace, *shalom*, nothing missing, nothing broken. First to them who believe. Everything I need, and everything you need, is in the gospel. Isn't that amazing? It's not out there, it's not in this, that, whatever. It's in the gospel and that can be in me, totally whole. Are you encouraged? Right, what we'll do now is split into twos and practise on each other. You can be resistant but not too much, OK? Jill and I will demonstrate first, and then the rest of you can split into pairs and then we'll practise and train.

[Terry] Hello, what's your name?

[Jill] Jill.

[Terry] Nice to meet you, I'm Terry. Good to see you. We're just doing some talking, if you've got a couple of minutes. Has anybody told you that God loves you? They have? Well that's great, that's good. Well, I'm here to encourage you today and tell you that God loves you, Jesus died for you and he's got a plan for your life. Do you mind if I just talk you through this? It's just four points. OK. The Bible says that God loves you; that we have all sinned – we've fallen short of the glory of God – but Jesus came and died for us so that we can be restored to God and have total forgiveness. Yes, that's right. The fourth point is that we need to decide to live for God and there's a prayer here we can pray. Would you mind if I just prayed a quick prayer with you? OK. I'll pray a quick prayer. 'Lord, I thank you for Jill, I pray you'll bless her, bless her family, give her long life, protect her and do good in her life. And I pray she'll come to know you and accept you quickly. Amen.' Would you like to accept Christ today? Would you like me to pray with you and for you? Would you like to receive forgiveness? Well, I've just explained it to you. God loves you . . .

[Jill] But I'm a good person.

[Terry] Well, this is what a lot of people say, but the Bible says we've all sinned and fallen short of the glory of God. The wages of sin is death but the gift of God is eternal life. So that's why we need forgiveness from sin. Jesus died for us. I can pray with you and for you right now and we'll pray and you can accept Christ. Good, yes, Amen. Just pray this prayer after me. 'Dear Lord Jesus, please forgive me, come into my life, help me live for you, fill me with your Holy Spirit, in the name of Jesus. Amen.' Wonderful, that's great. Well I'd like to give you this; you can take that with you and we can also invite you to our local church. We have a meeting tonight.

Give Jill a round of applause, she's just got saved again. OK, Jill's going to demonstrate on me now.

[Jill] What I'd probably say is to just check with someone that it's OK to touch them. Terry knew it was OK to take my hand but when you don't know the person, just always ask first. You can be bold and say, 'Is it OK to touch your arm?' If you don't feel like you want to, then just do what you feel comfortable with and whatever the other person feels comfortable with.

[Jill] Hello there.

[Terry] Hey up.

[Jill] You don't sound like you're from London? You're from up North. We like people from up North. Can I ask you a question? Did you know that God loves you, Jesus died for you and has got a plan for your life? Has anyone ever told you that? That's good. Would you like to know more? Well, the Bible says that we've all sinned and all fallen short of God's measure, that we've missed the mark. Well, let me just show you this. I'm going to give you this as a free gift. Says here a big heart, because God loves me, but it also says a big X – I have sinned, which means we've fallen short of the glory of God, but Jesus has made a way because he died for us! But now we've got to decide to live for God. Do you mind if I pray for you? Is it OK that I just put my hand on your arm? 'Lord, we thank you for Terry, for his life. We thank you that you want to bless him and his family and bless everything he does in the name of Jesus. We thank you for it. Come and touch him today, Lord, and I hope he accepts you quickly.' Would you like the gift of salvation? Then we're going to say this pray, the prayer on the script.